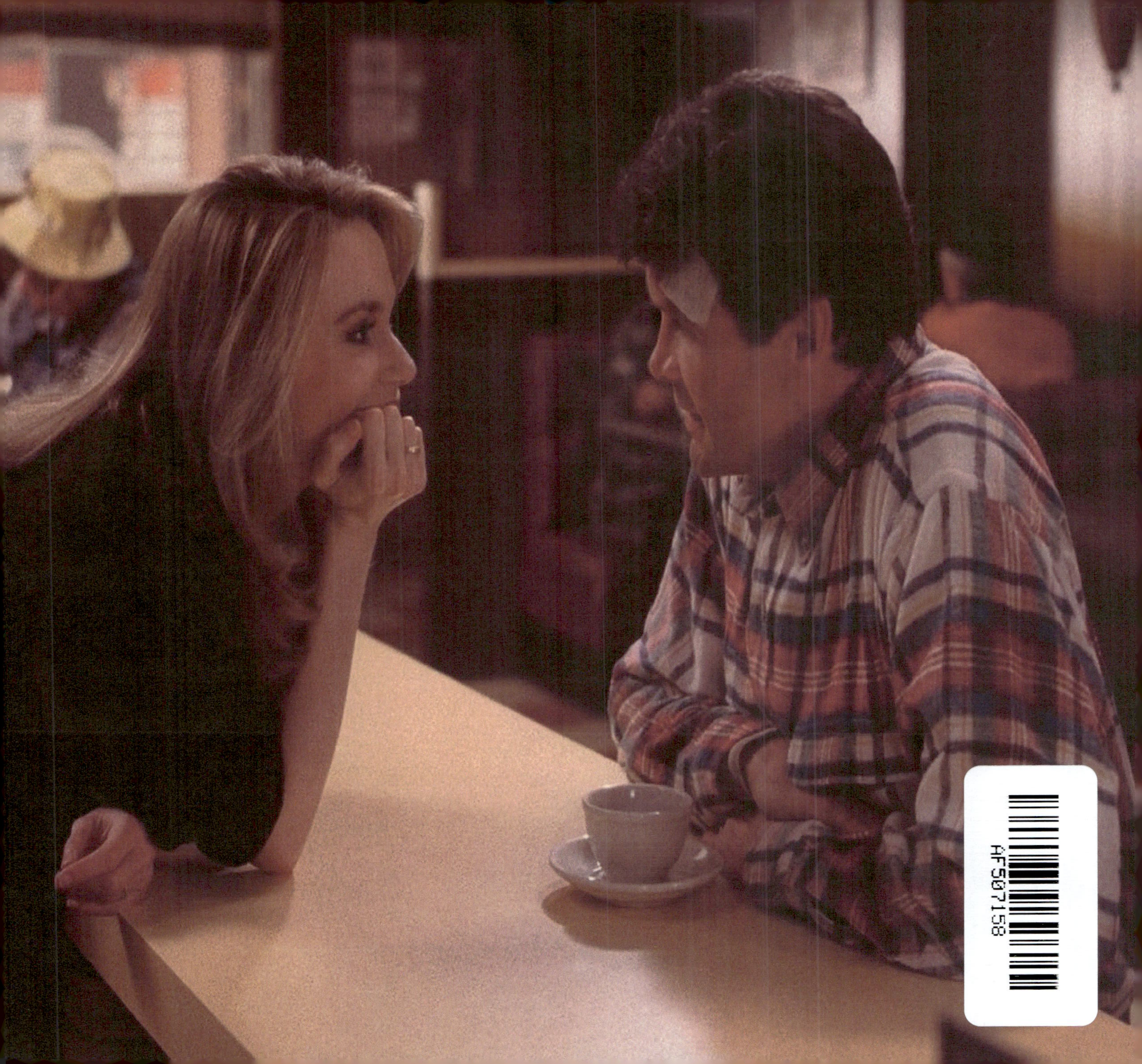

AF507158

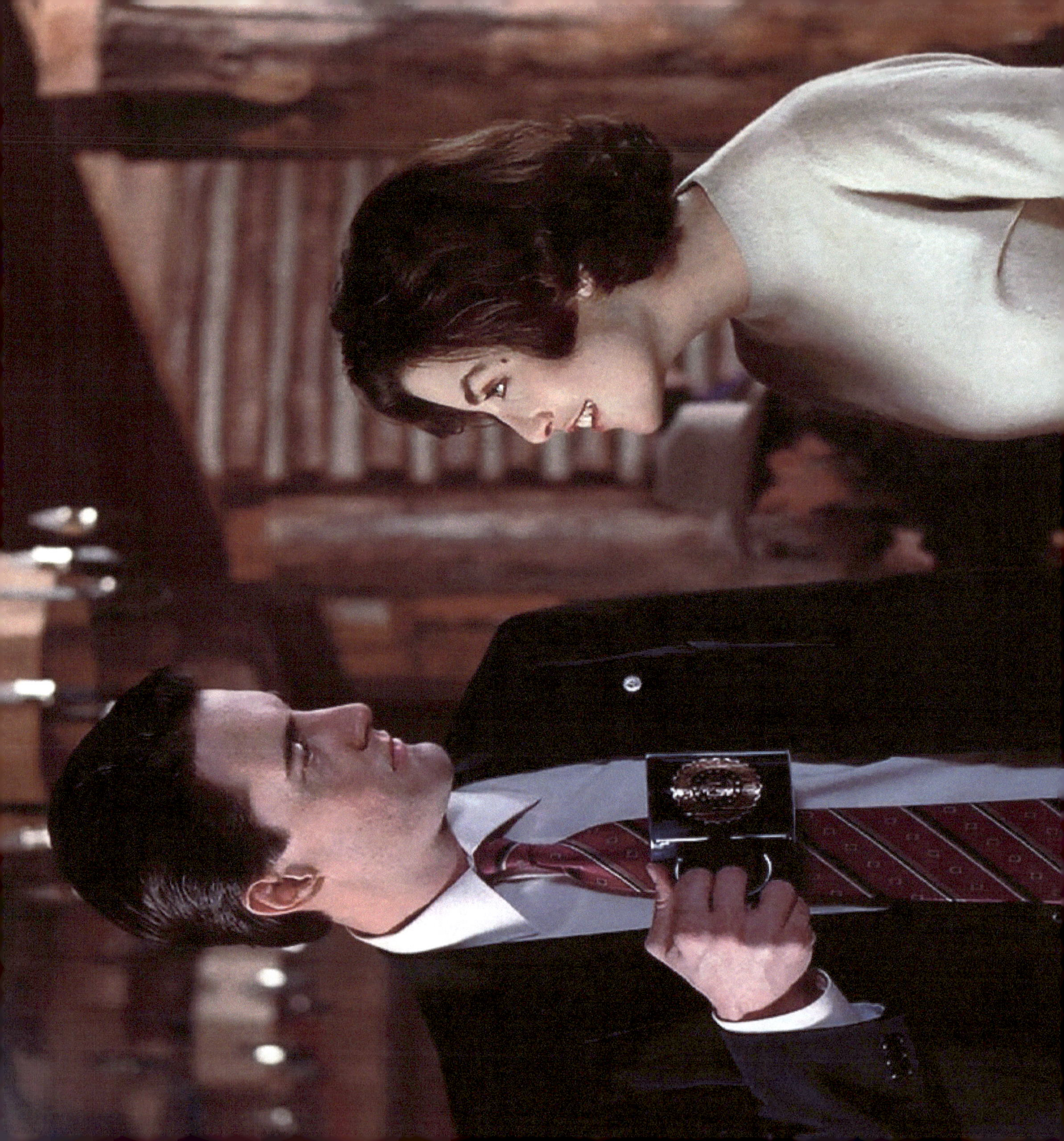

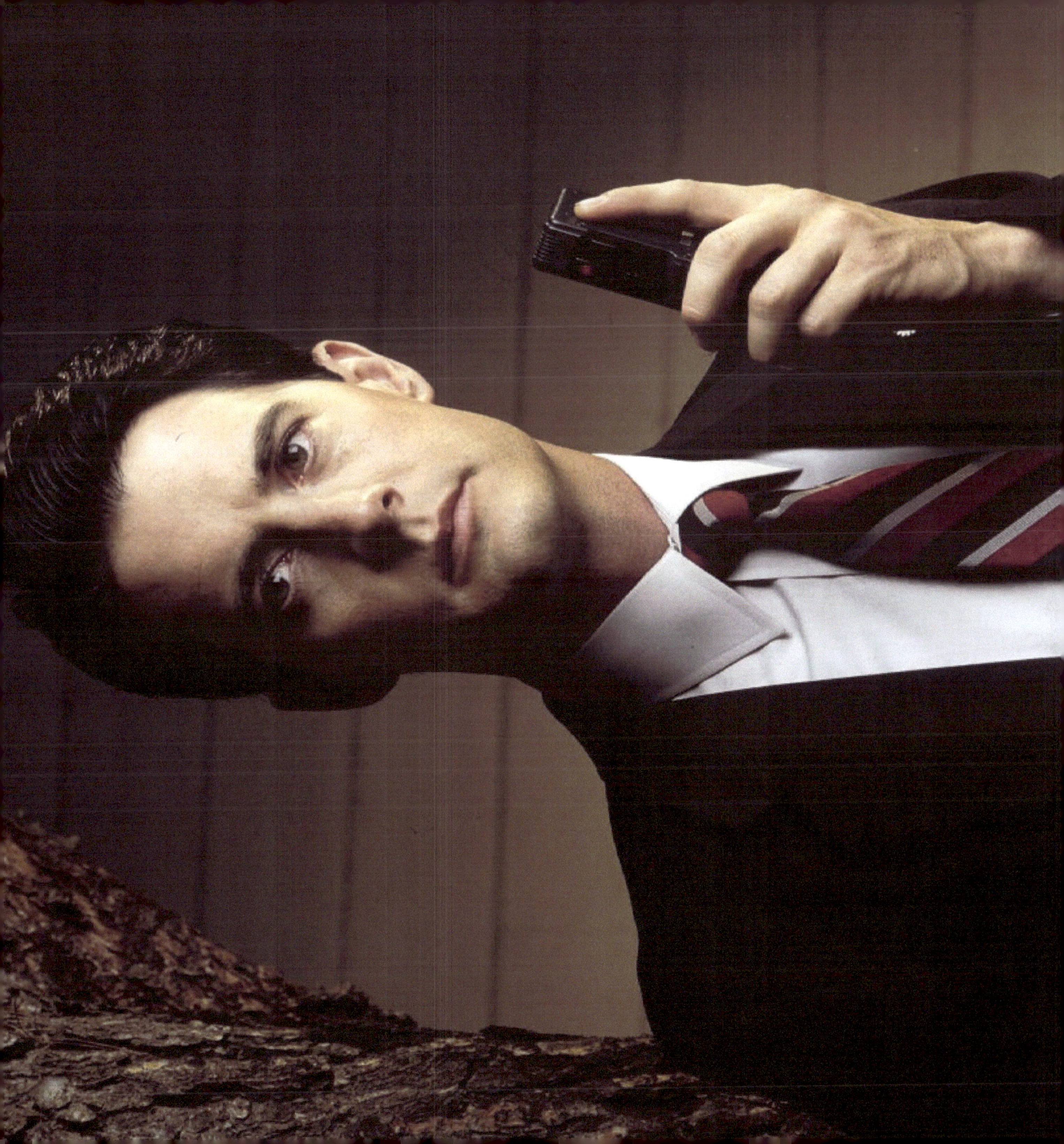

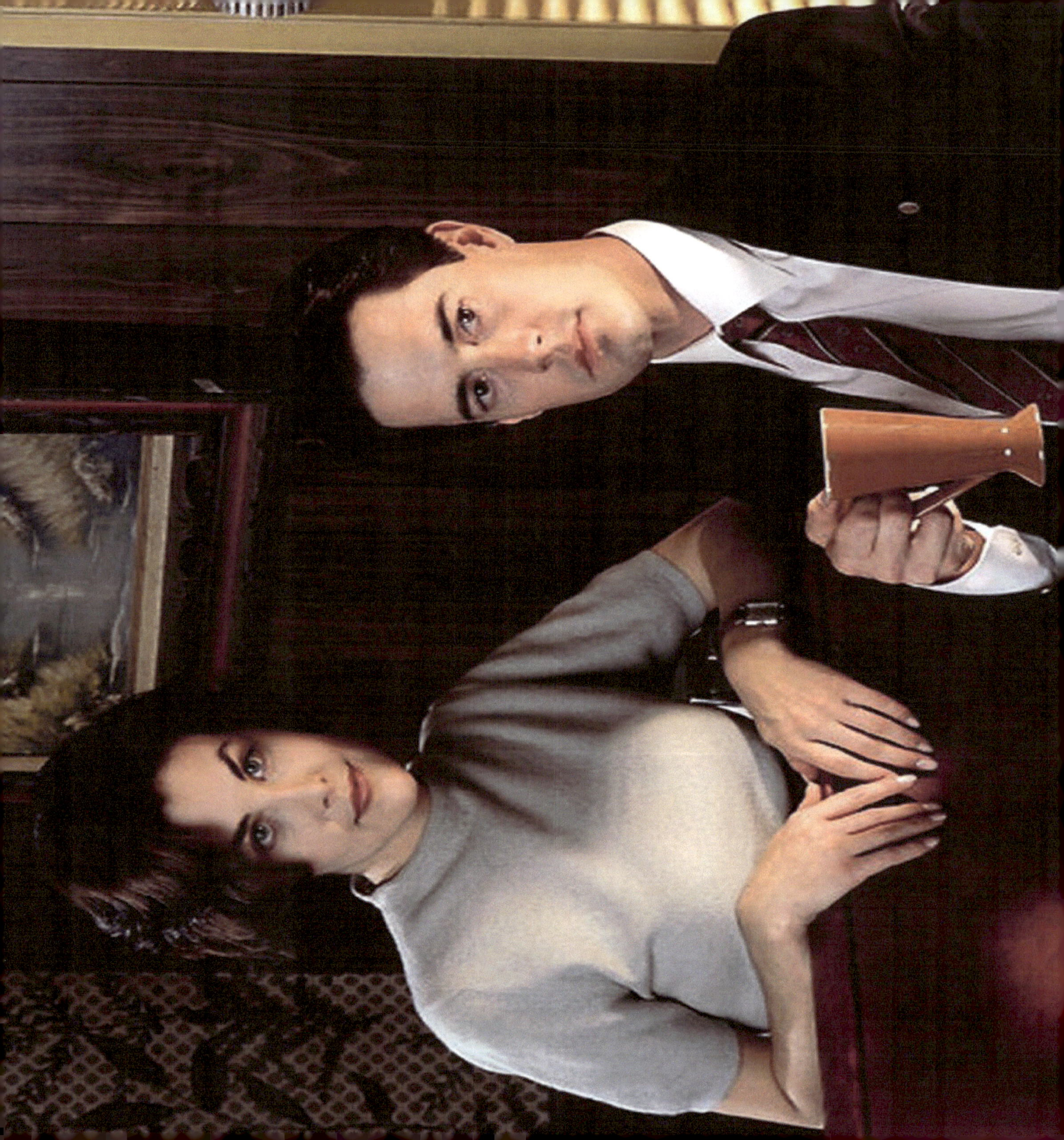

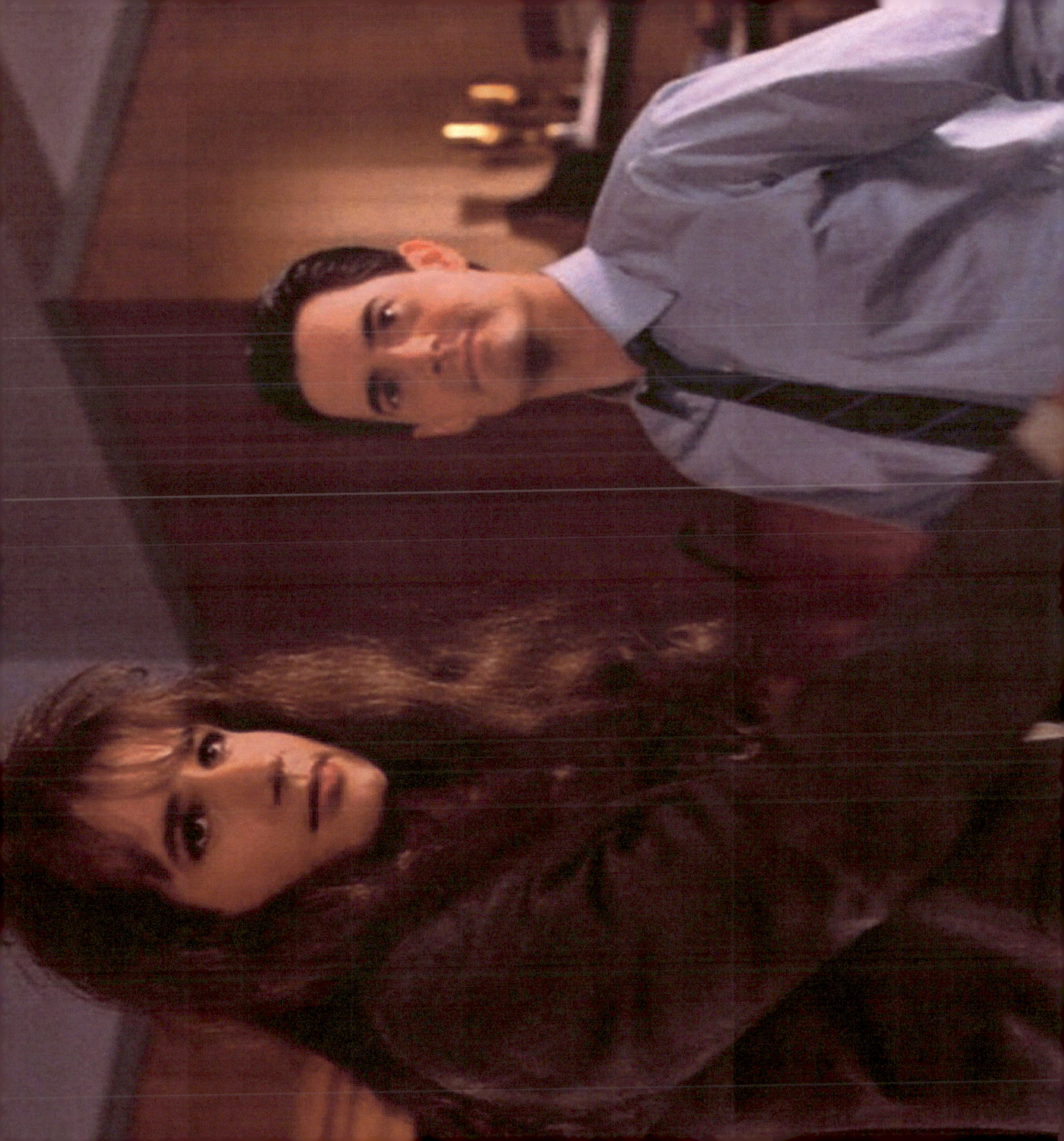

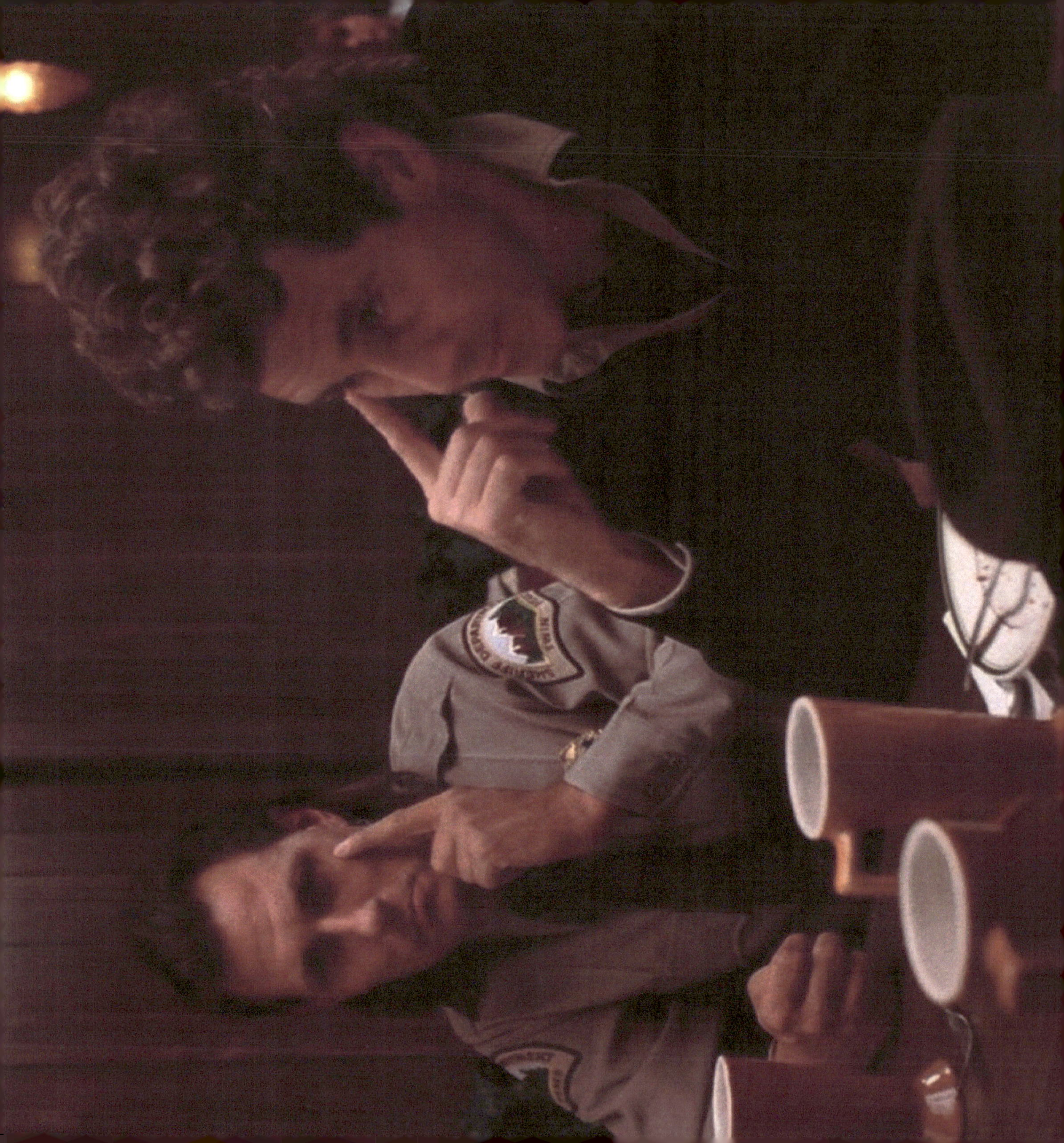

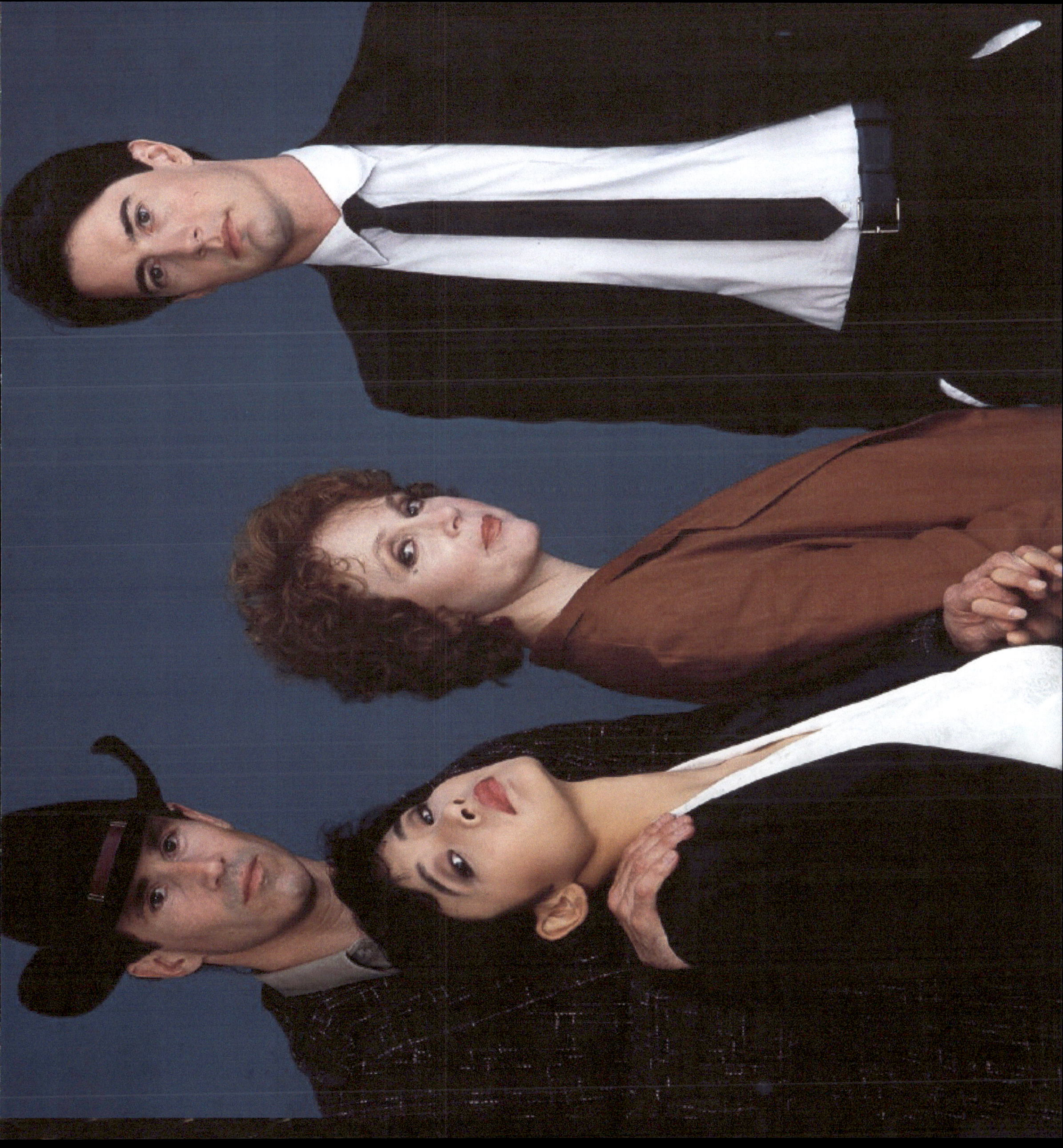

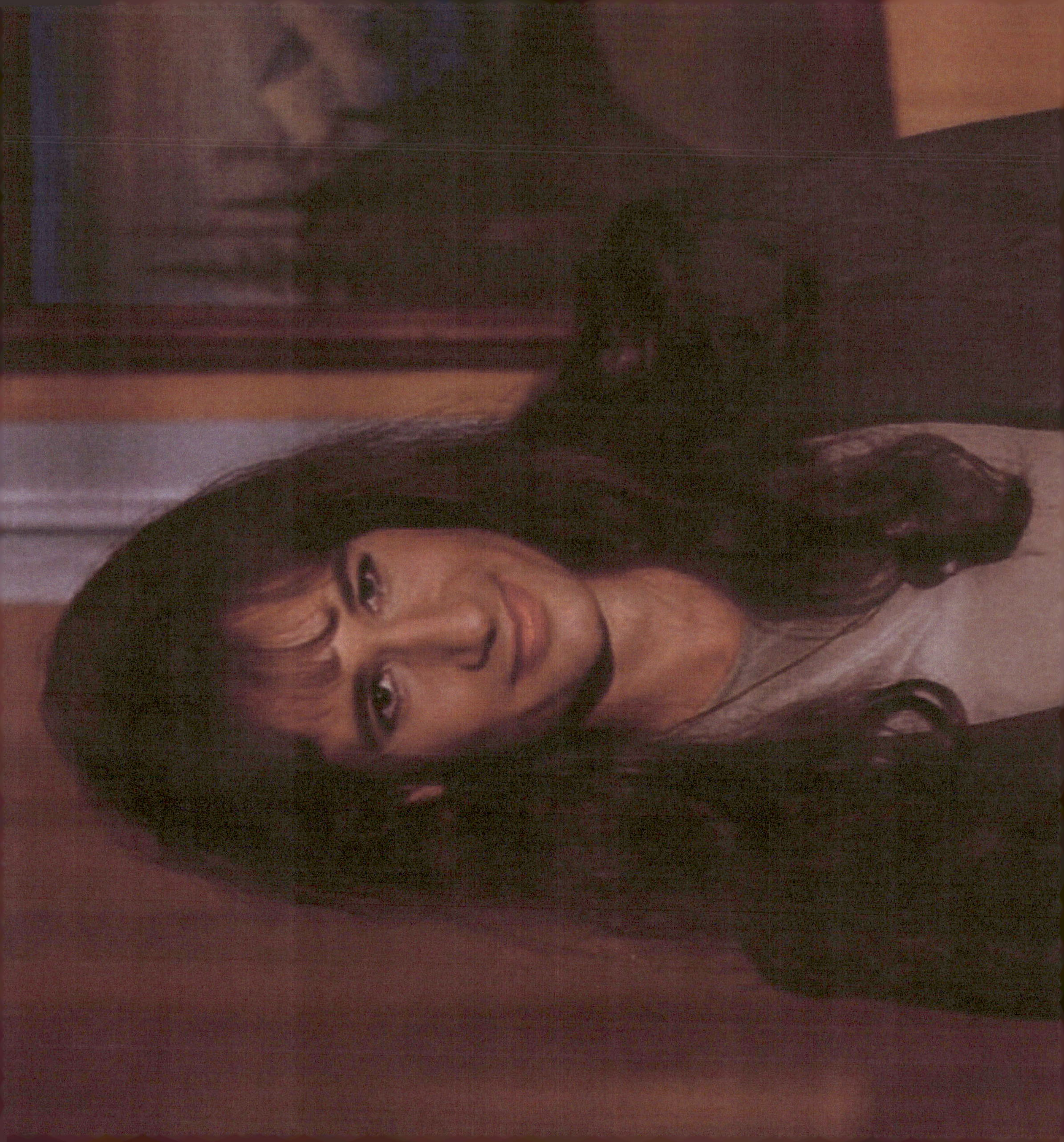

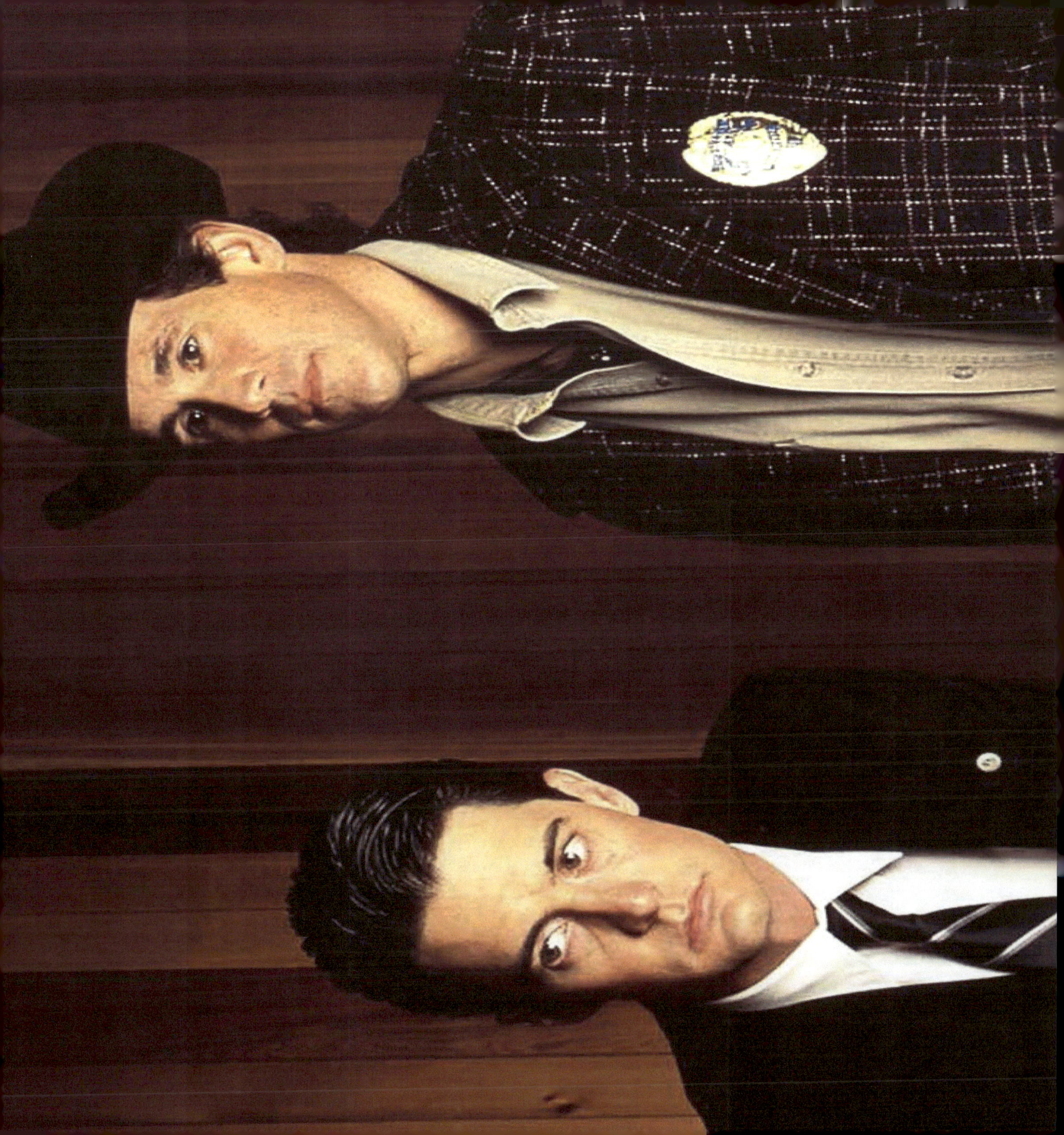

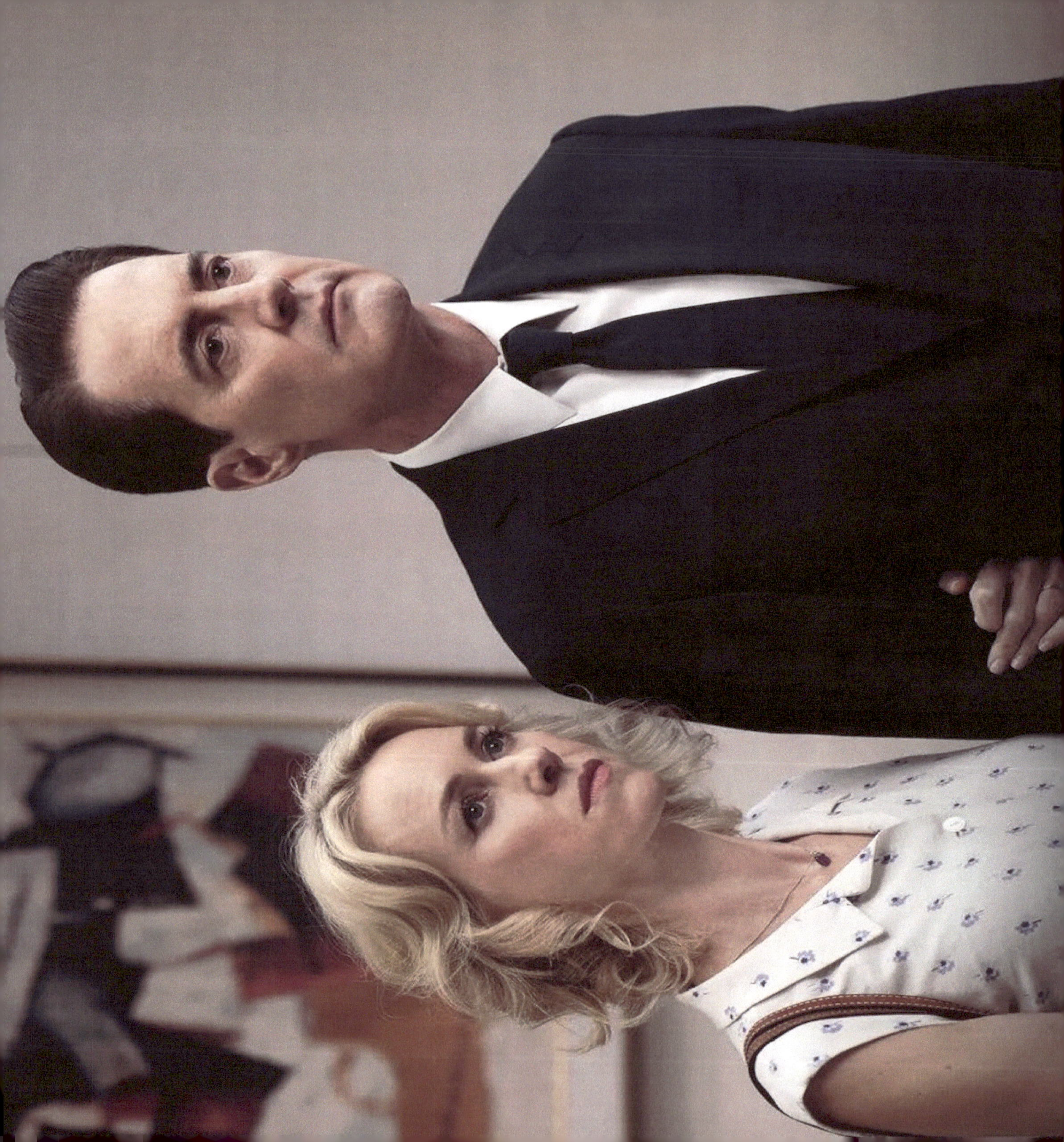

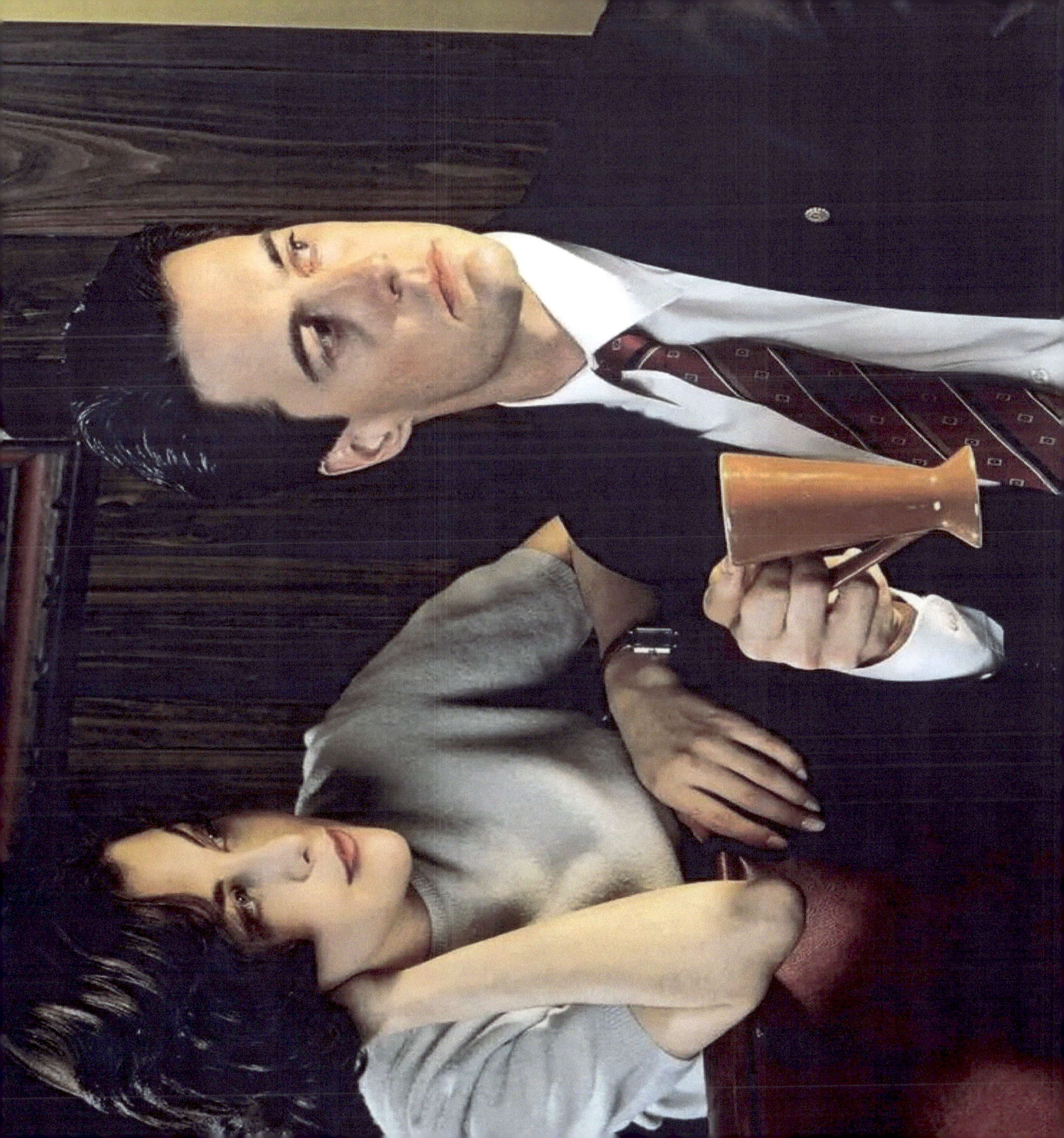

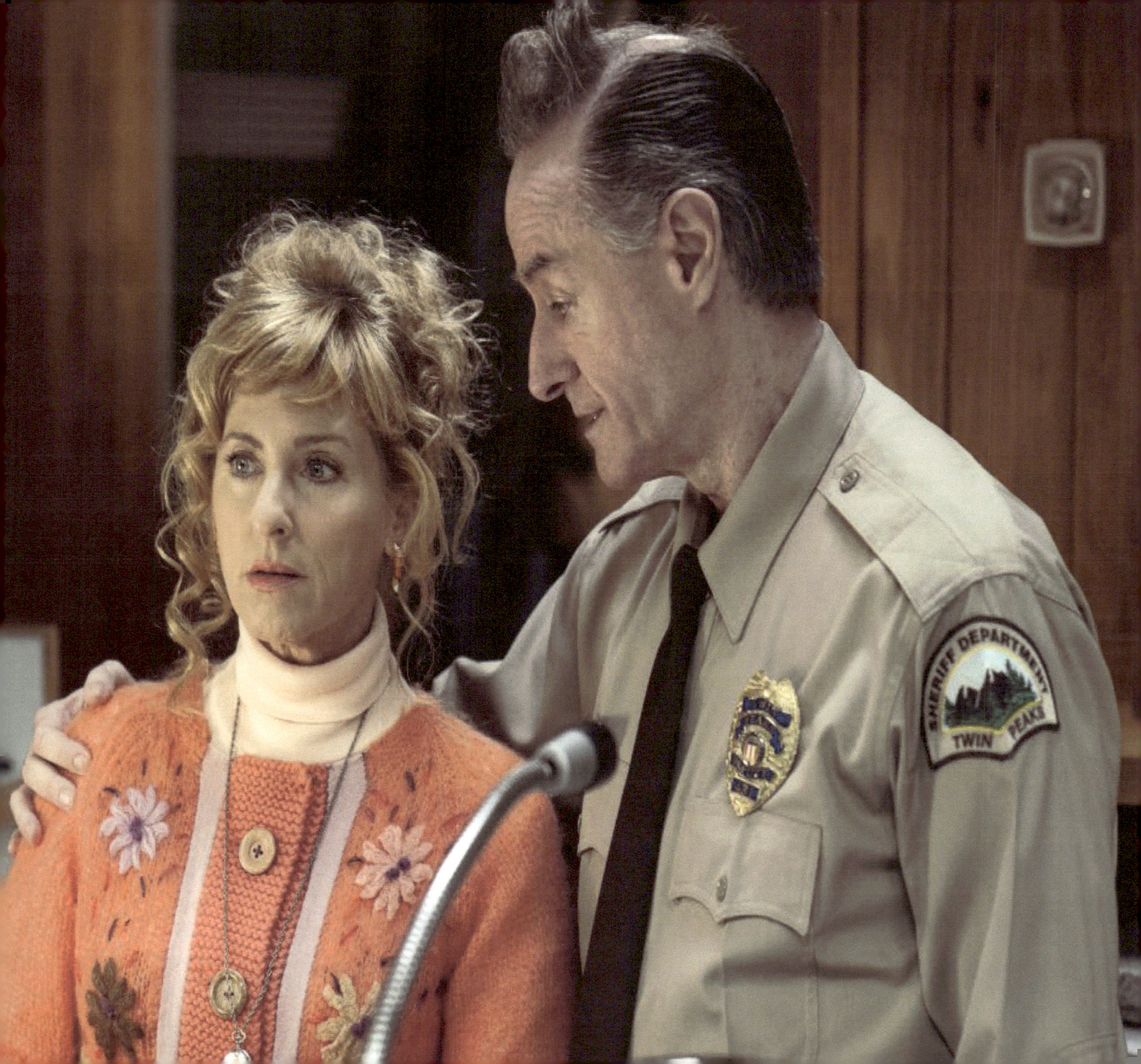

SHERIFF DEPARTMENT
TWIN PEAKS

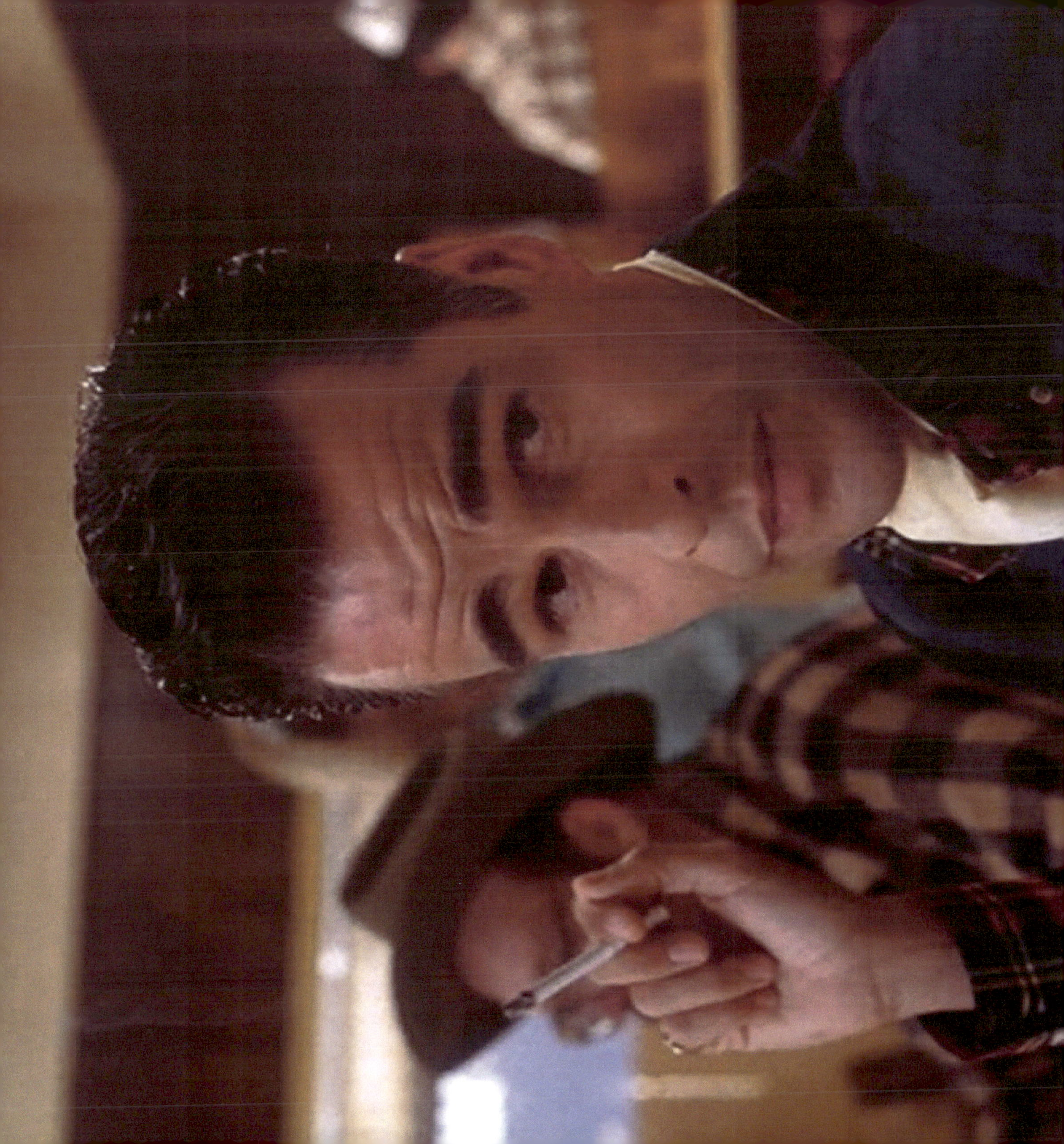

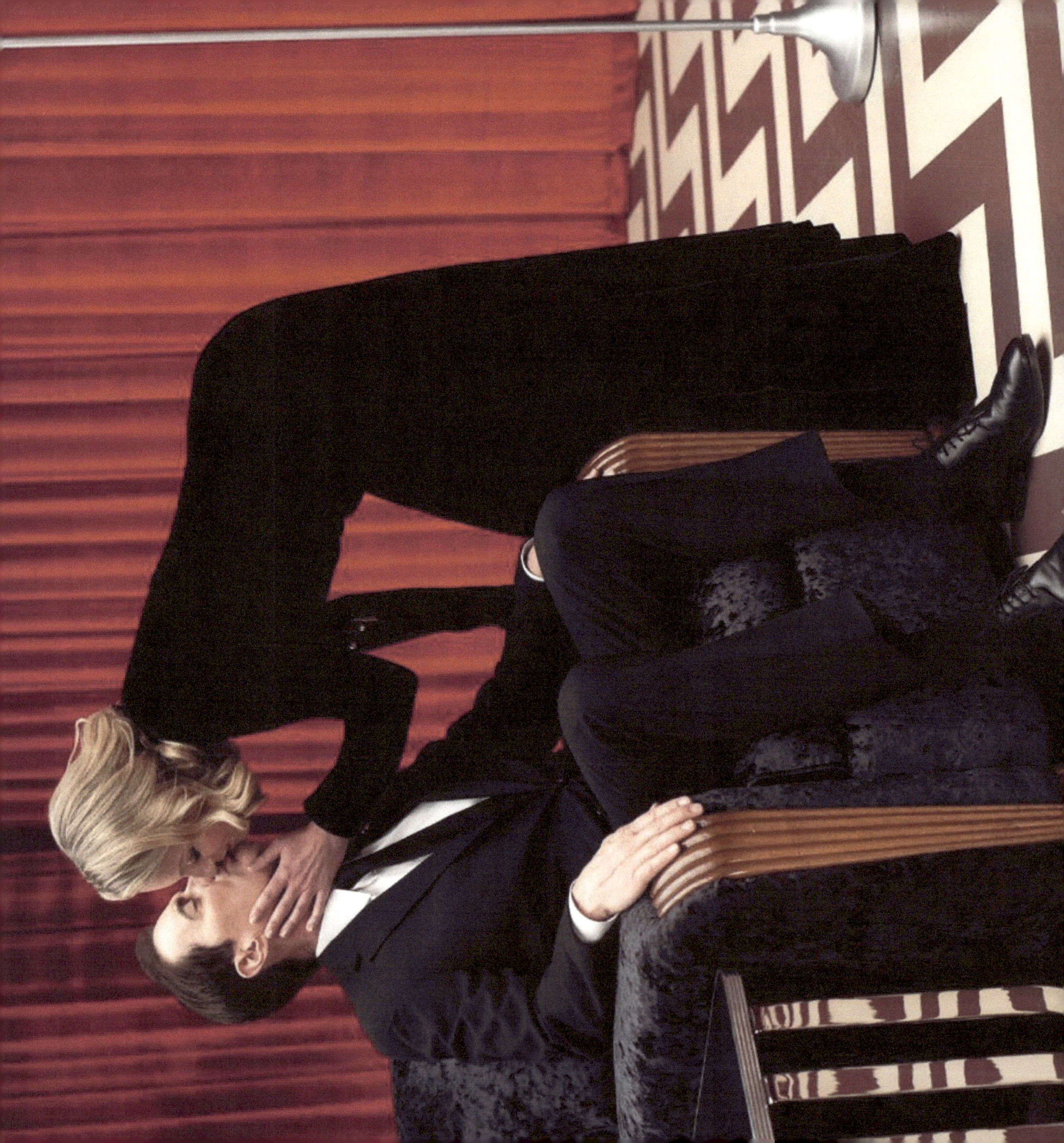

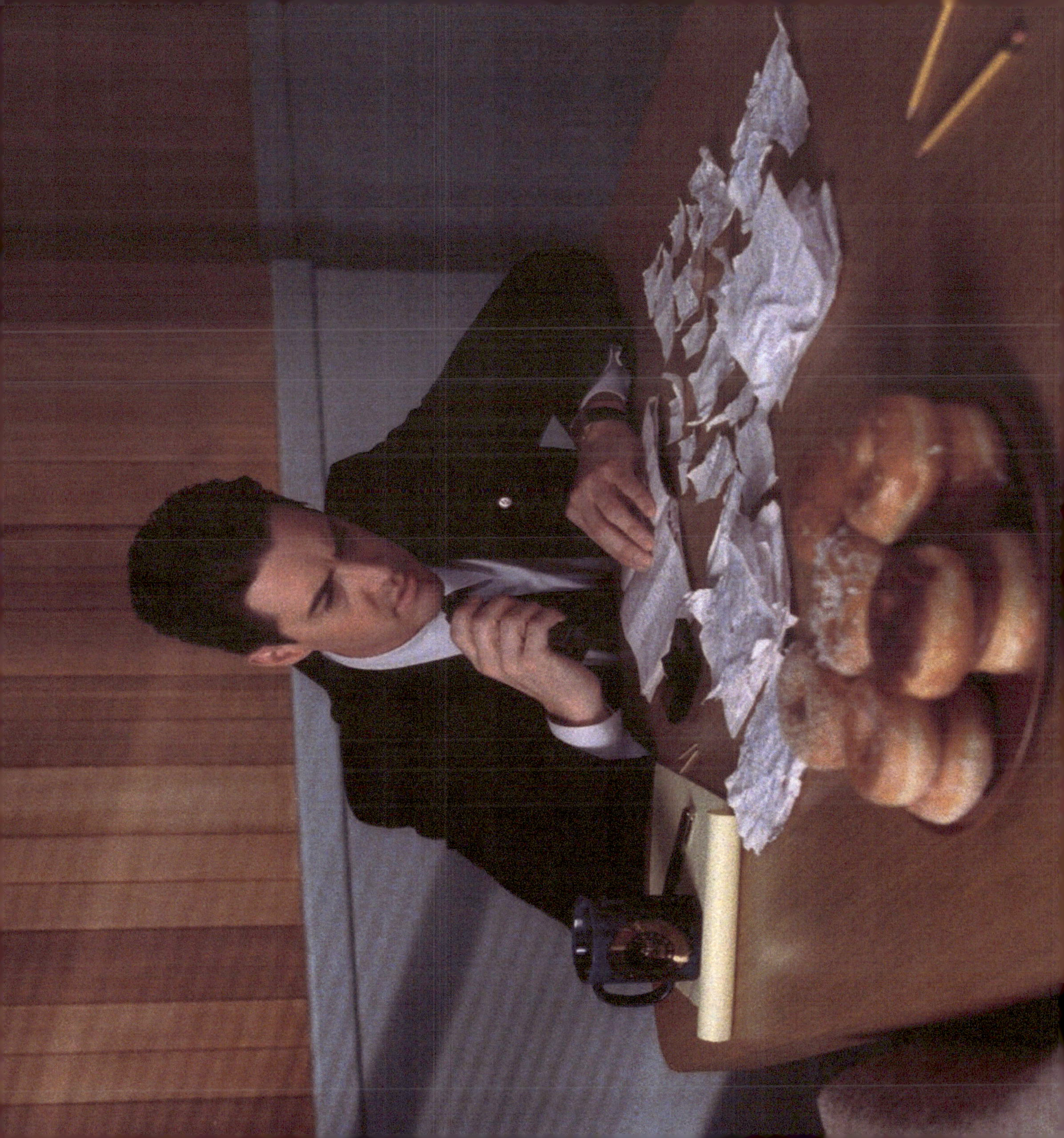

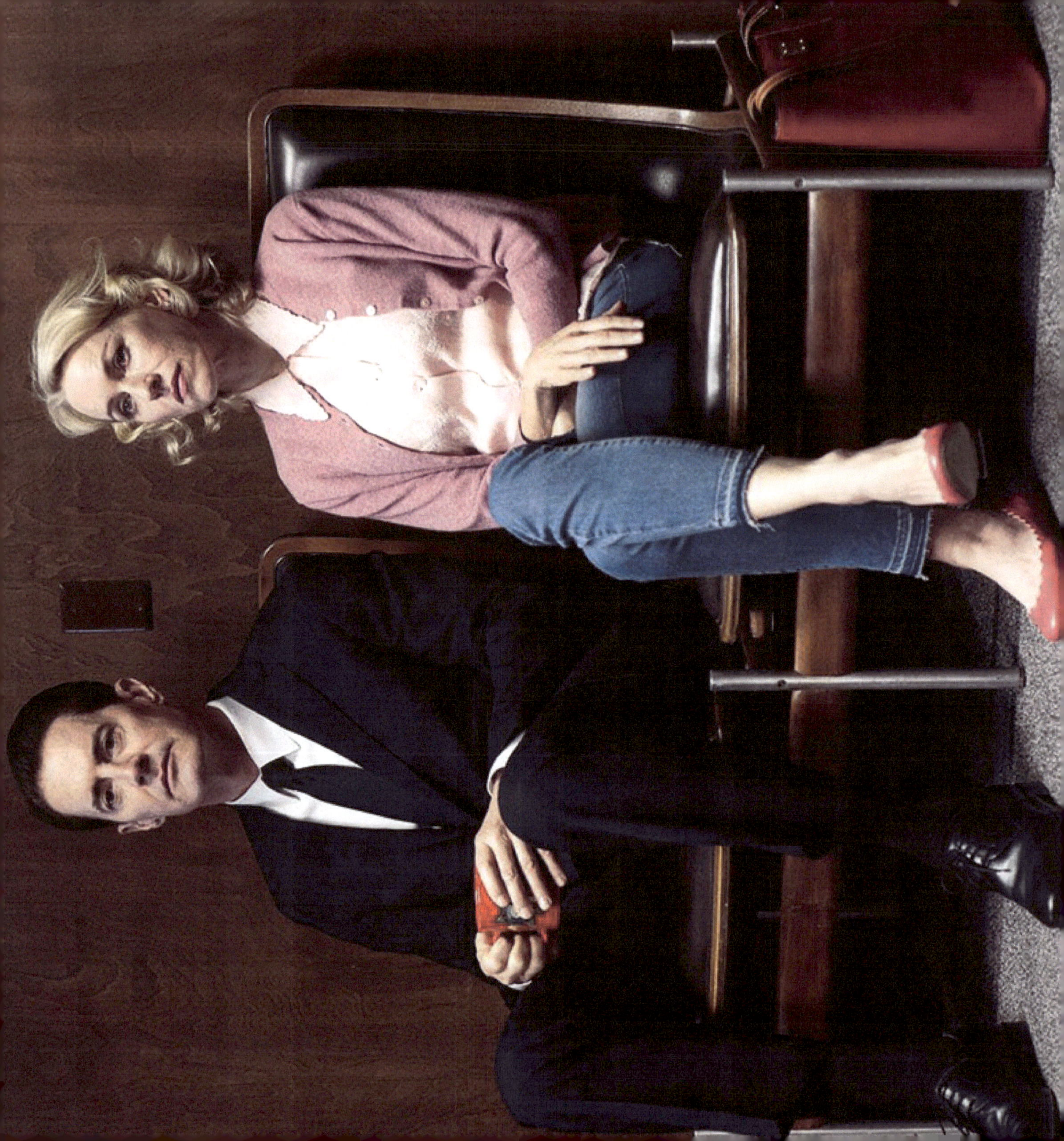

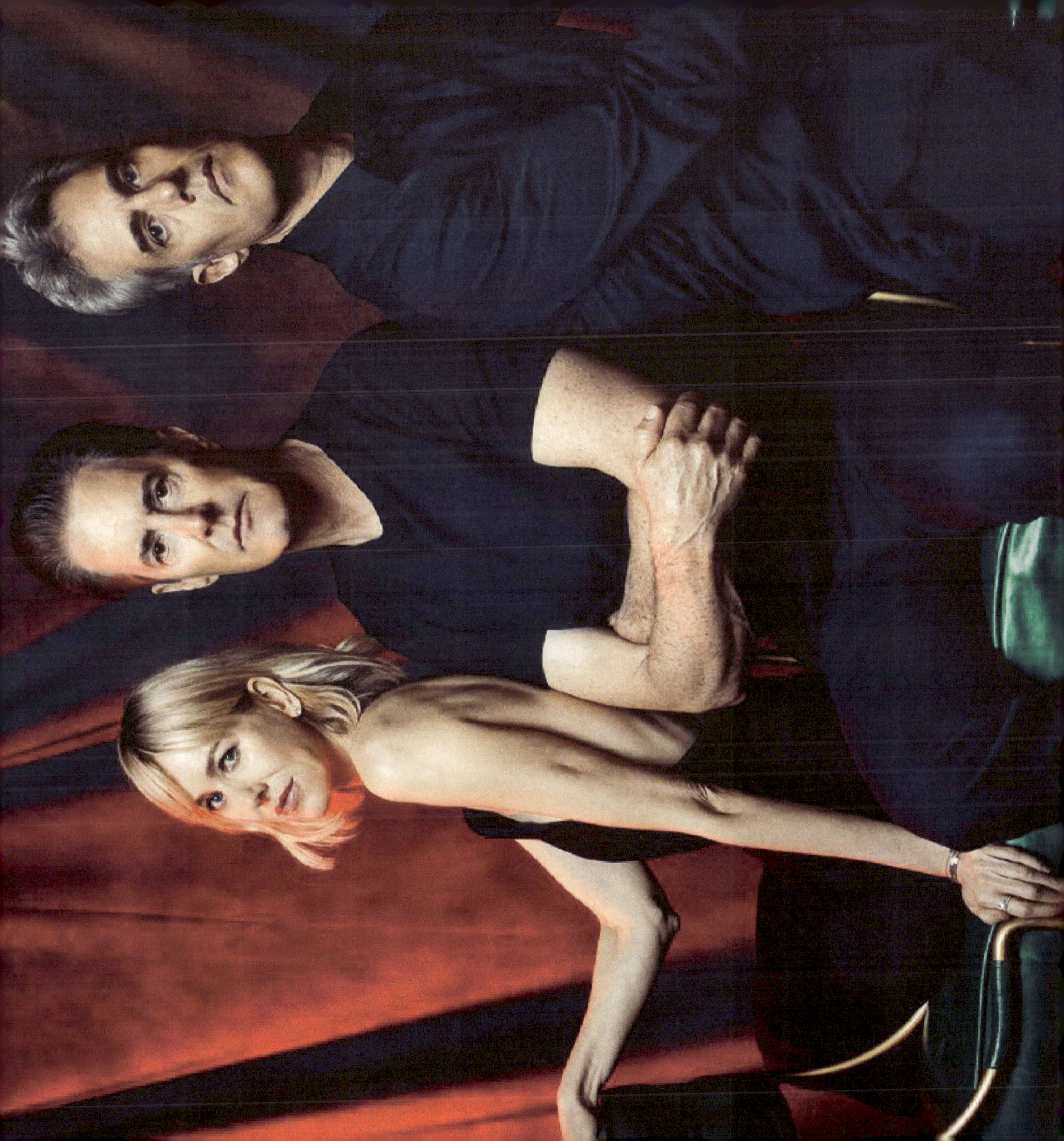

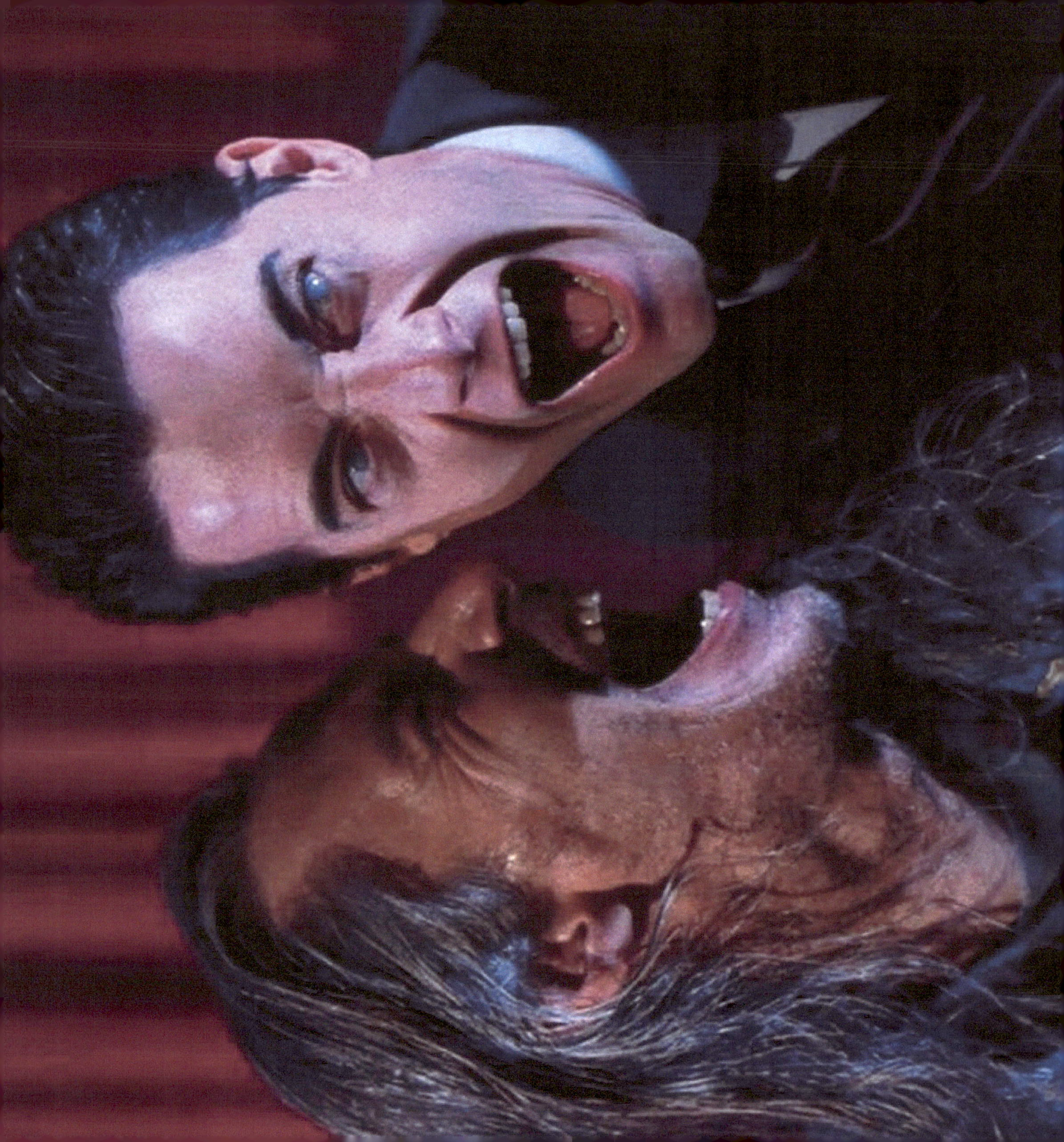

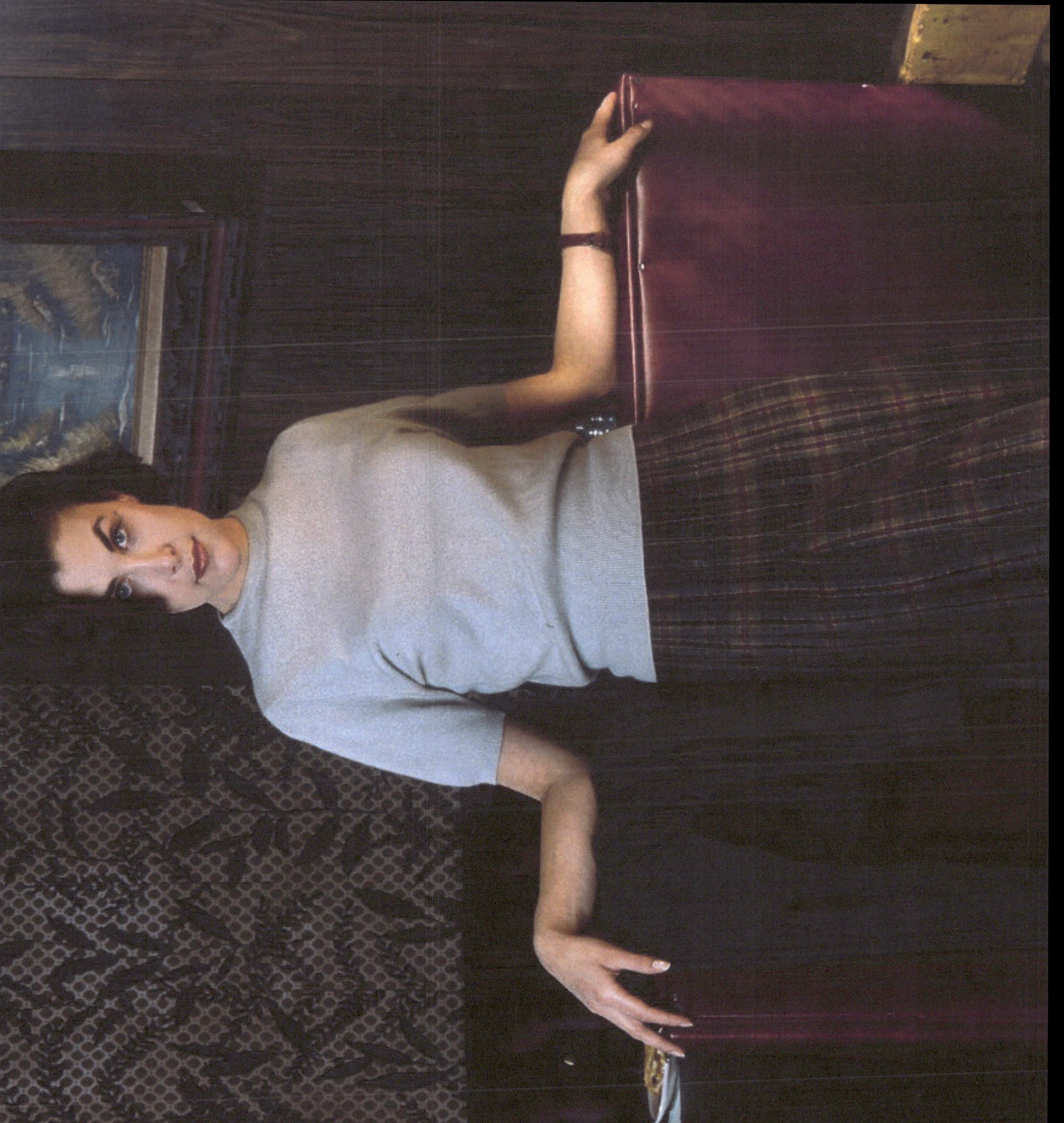

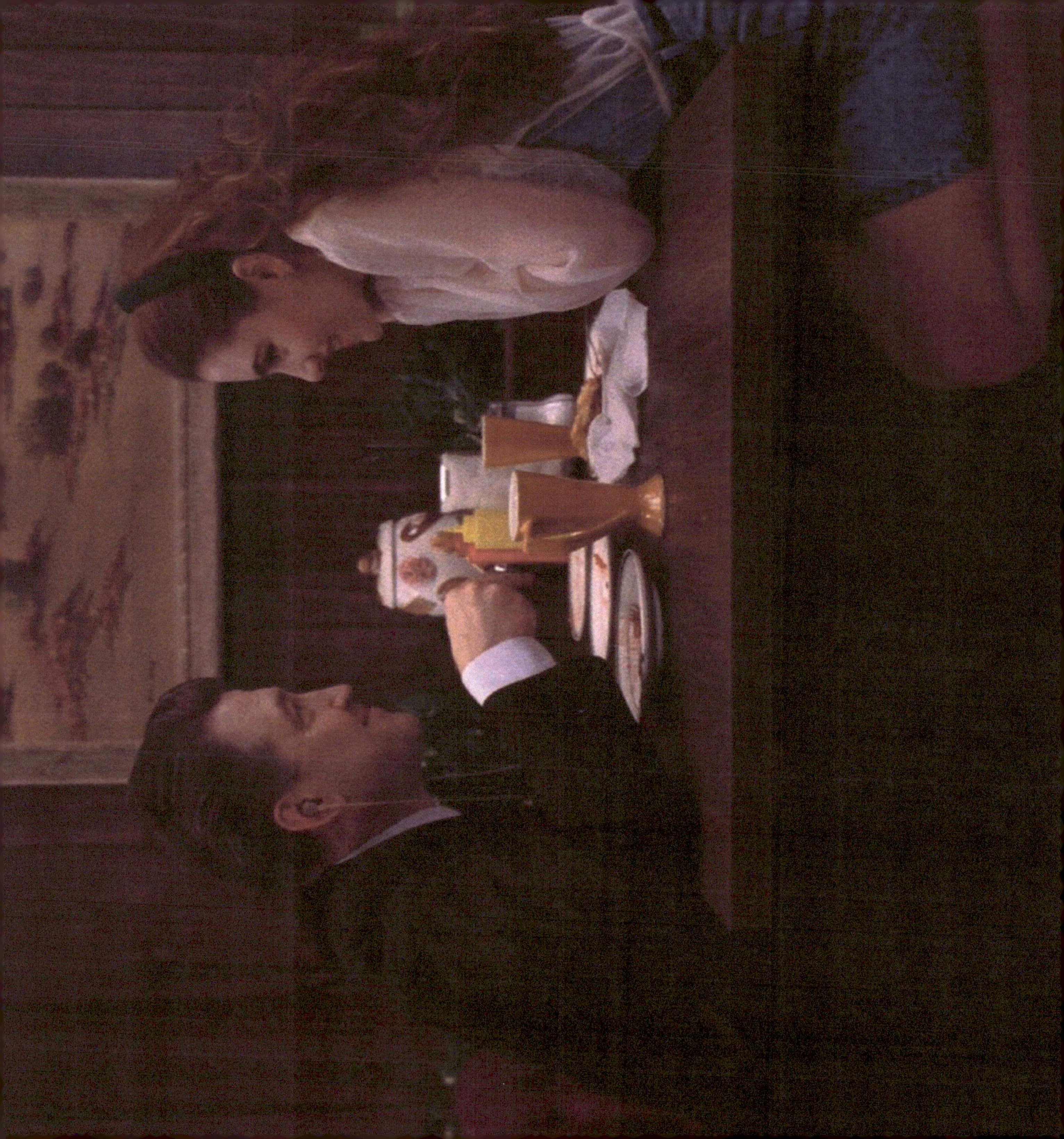

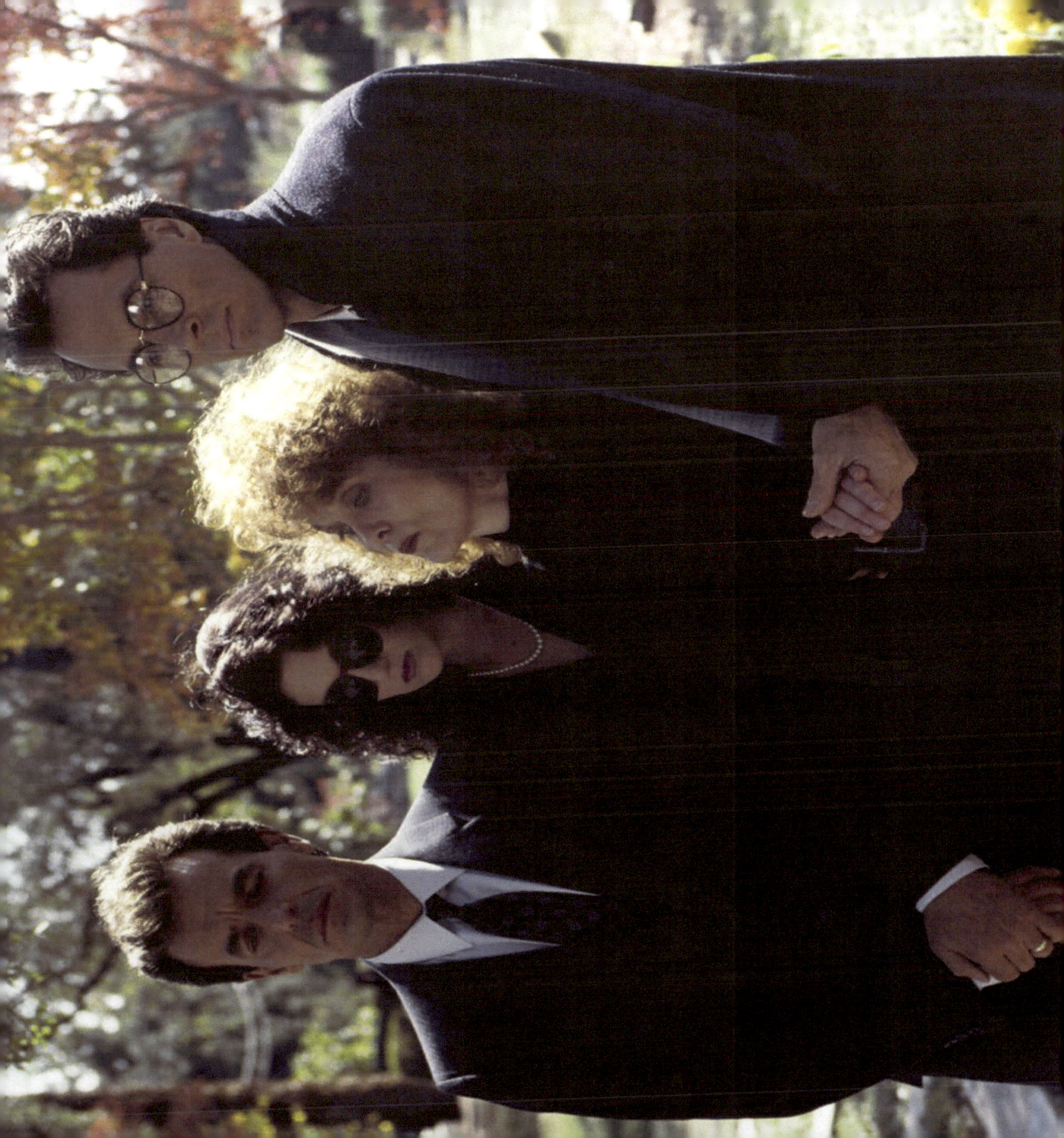

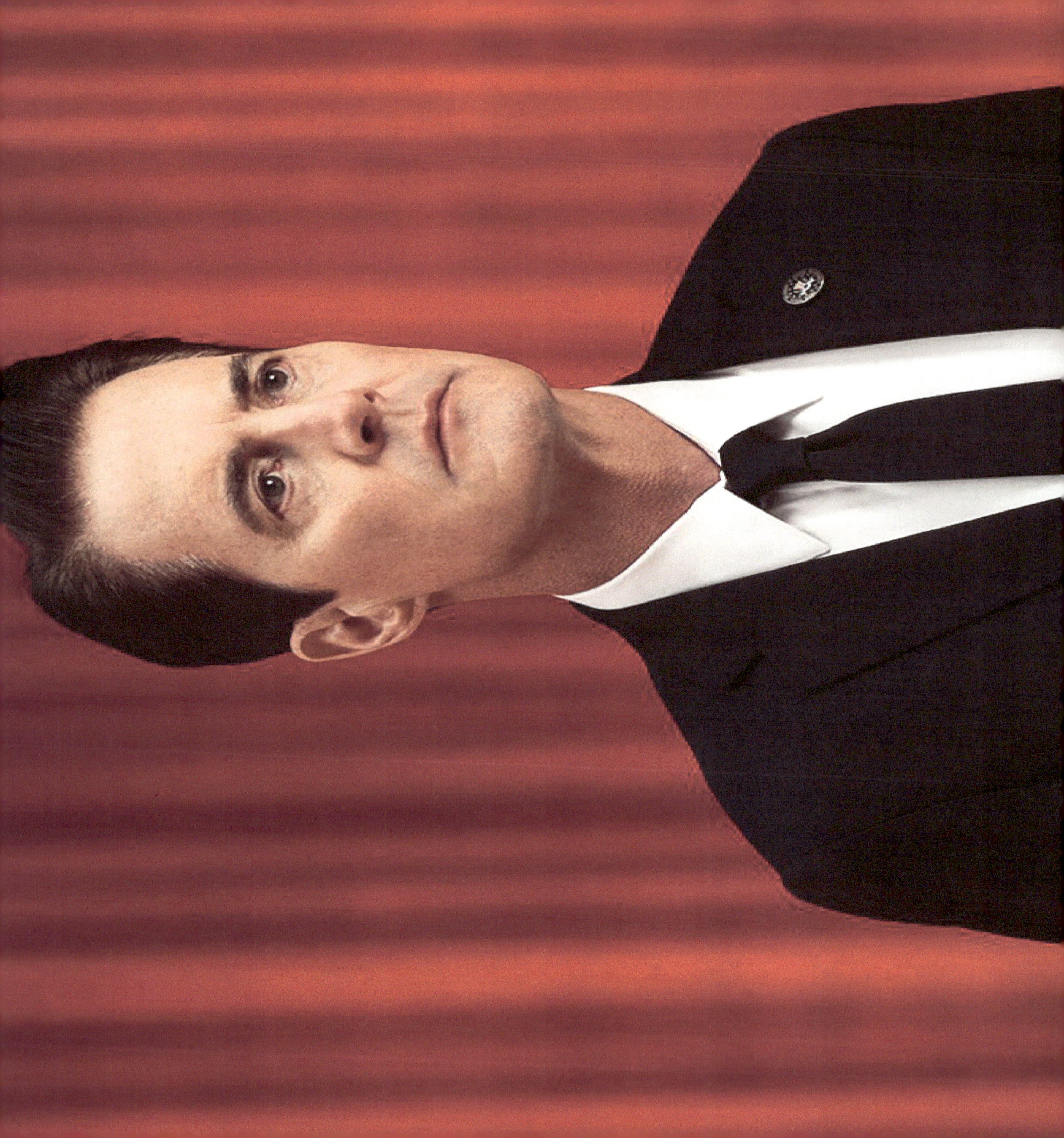

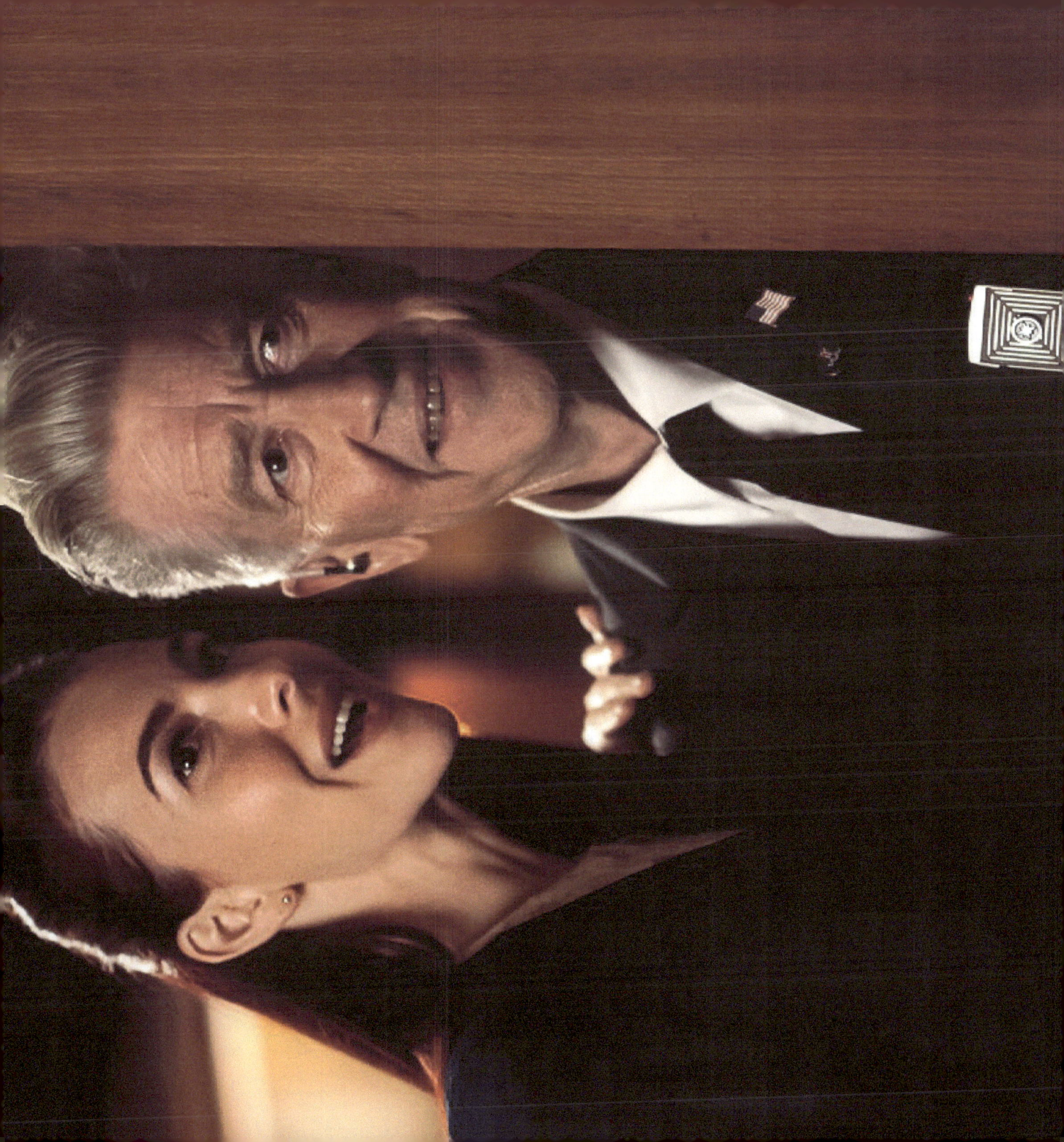

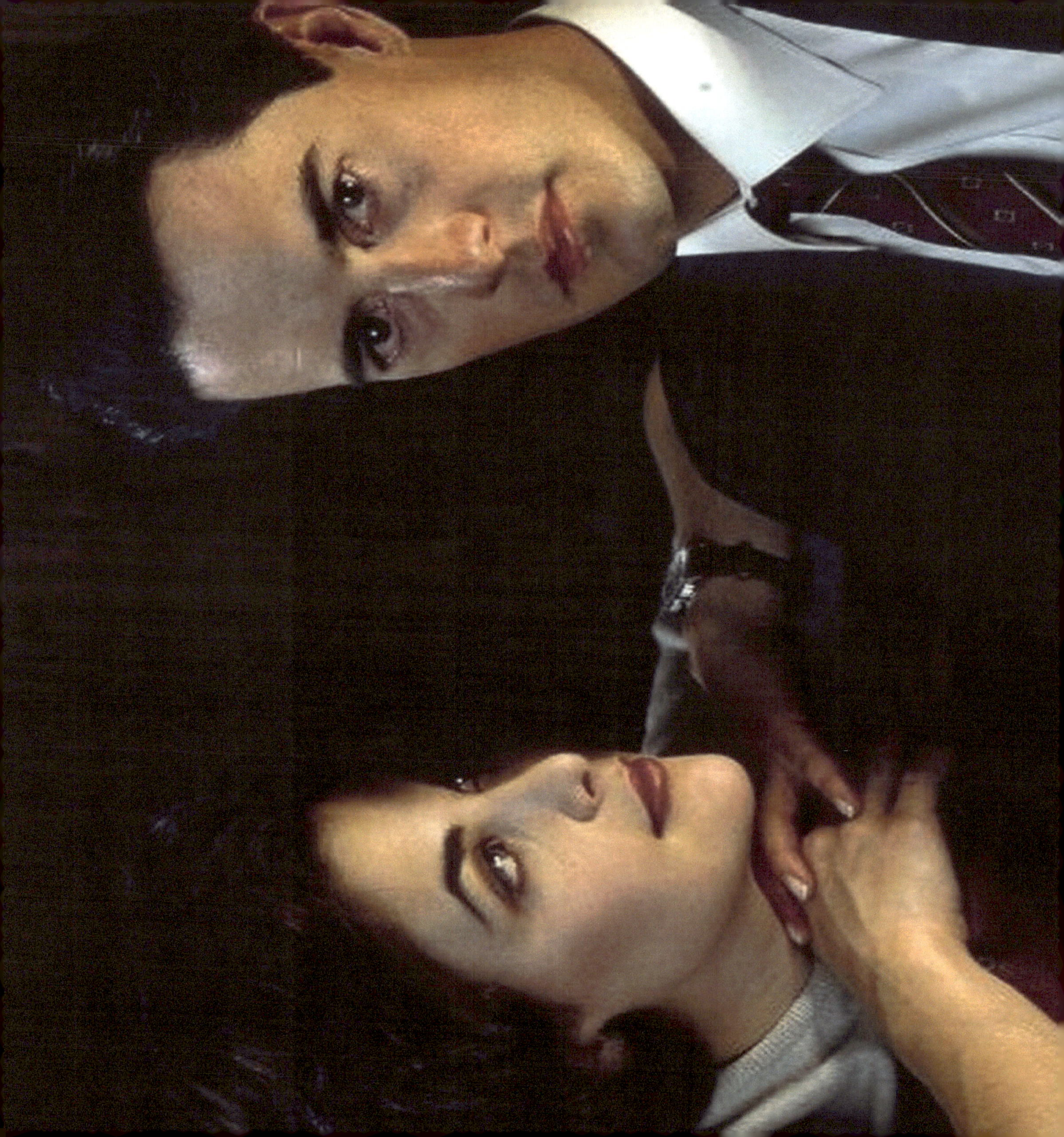

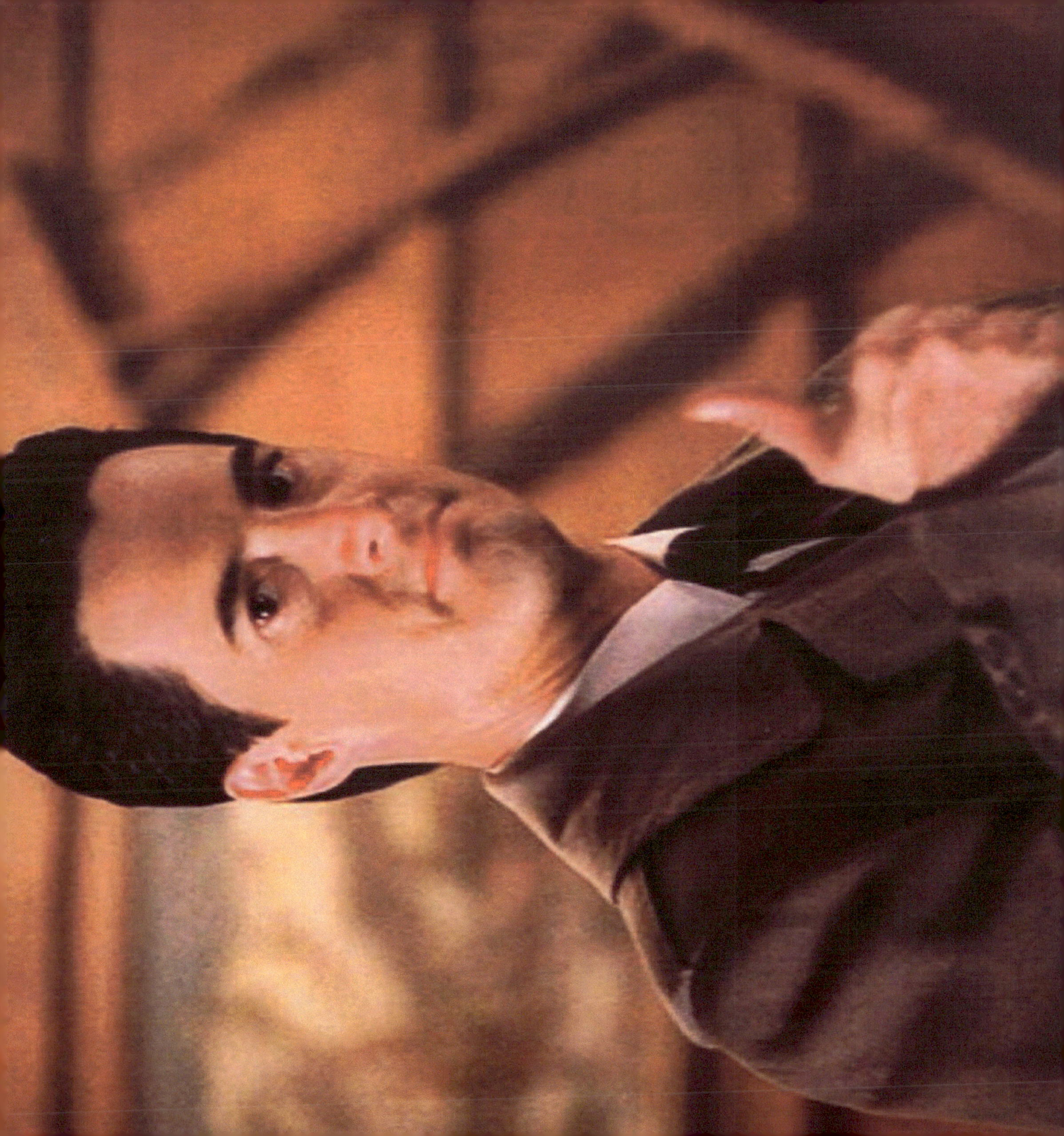

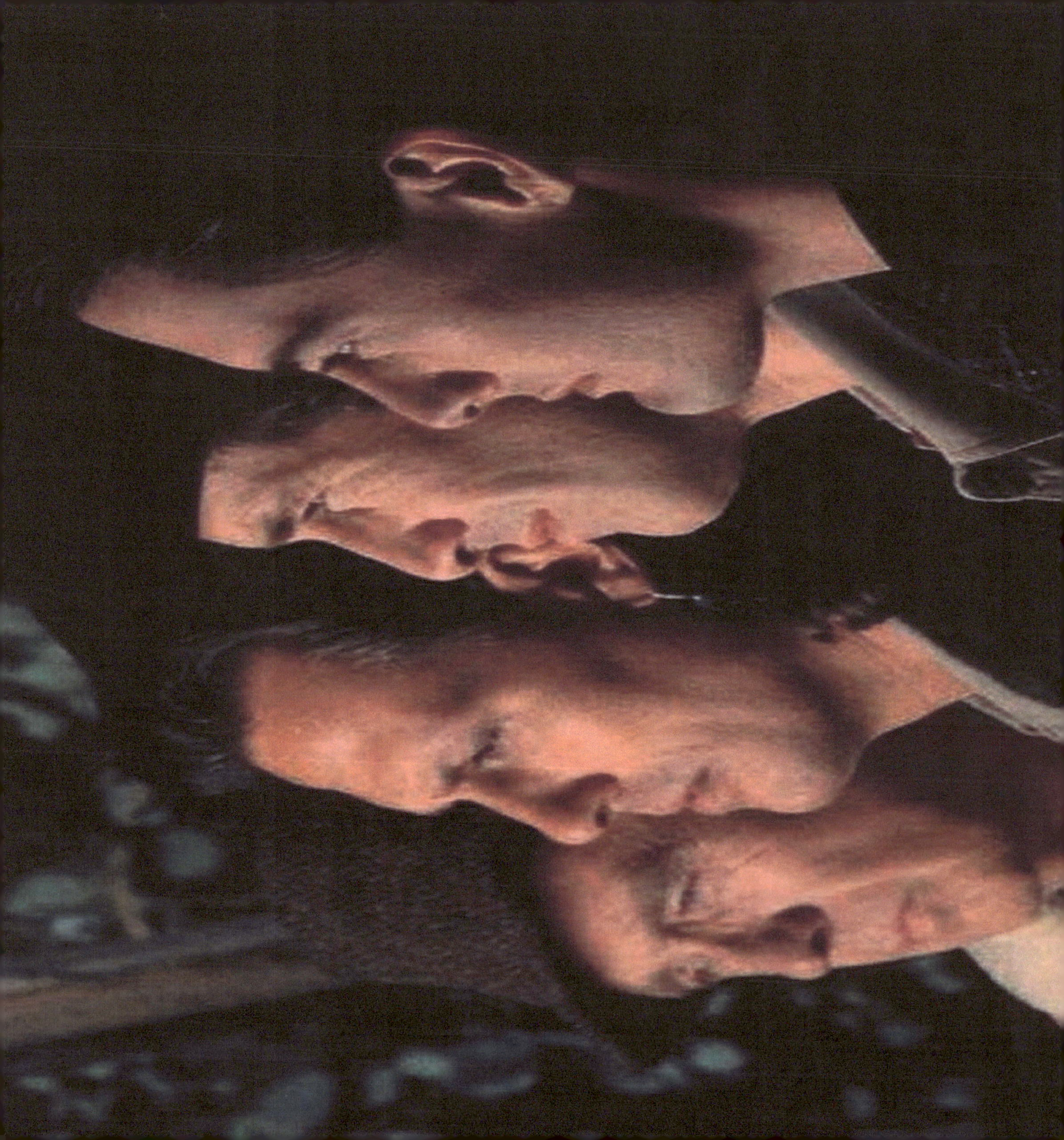